ABSTRACT

I0429220

The stationing of U.S. military personnel in South Korea is viewed by many as a Cold War hold over that serves no contemporary purpose. Reasons given for ending the U.S. military presence in South Korea are that these forces are no longer needed to defend South Korea against North Korea, the cost of maintaining U.S. forces in South Korea is too high, the commitment of U.S. forces in Korea limits U.S. strategic flexibility, and rising South Korean anti-Americanism. This paper examines these concerns as well as the role U.S. forces play in providing security on the Korean Peninsula and stability in the Asian-Pacific Region. It then examines three courses of action the U.S. could adopt while still fulfilling its commitment to the US-ROK Mutual Defense Treaty. The conclusion is that the U.S. should maintain current force levels in South Korea. The continued unambiguous resolve and commitment of the U.S. to the stability of the Asia-Pacific and its allies remains a prudent, cost-effective constant. U.S. forces in South Korea are part of the strong U.S.–ROK alliance and serve a vital purpose today – their presence promotes stability and continued regional security. This not only benefits the U.S. but also the other nations of the region and the world.

U.S. TROOPS STATIONED IN SOUTH KOREA, ANACHRONISTIC?

For the last 60 years South Korea has been one of the United States' strongest and most reliable allies. The focus of this alliance 'formed in blood' during the Korean War has evolved over the years as the South Korean economy has expanded, the capacity of South Korean military forces has increased, and the Cold War ended. Today, the changing global environment places the alliance at a pivotal point. The North Korean threat to stability, globalization, international terrorism, the rise of China, U.S. economic concerns, and the desire of the Republic of Korea (ROK) to have greater control of its armed forces are all factors the alliance must address. While it is certain the alliance with the ROK will continue to remain vital to the United States, we must reexamine the need for stationing U.S. troops in South Korea. Do these U.S troops serve a vital role today in support of the alliance or are they simply an anachronistic holdover from the Cold War?

Background

History of US Troop Commitment to South Korea. United States military personnel have served in South Korea since the conclusion of World War II in 1945 when the U.S. accepted the surrender of Japanese military forces south of the 38th Parallel. Initially, American officers served as commanders of the South Korean Constabulary. Soon thereafter, they became advisors in the Korean Military Advisory Group after the Republic of Korea formed the Ministry of Defense and established the ROK Army in 1948.[1] There were 510 U.S. service members serving in this capacity on 25 June, 1950 when South Korea was attacked by North Korea.[2]

Following this attack, the U.S. quickly decided to commit combat forces in the defense of South Korea. This decision was made against the backdrop of the Cold War with the Soviet Union since South Korea itself held little U.S. strategic interest. As recently as 1947, the U.S. Joint Chiefs of Staff (consisting of Admiral Leahy, Admiral Nimitz, General Eisenhower, and General Spaatz) concluded there were no U.S. strategic interests in Korea.[3] Additionally, at a speech at the National Press Club on 12 January, 1950 Secretary of State Dean Acheson stated the U.S. would not pledge to provide military protection to the ROK "because it was outside the 'defensive perimeter' of the United States."[4] It was, however, in the strategic interests of the U.S. to stop the spread of communism through its policy of containment. Following closely on the heels of the communist victory in China in 1949, the U.S. feared that if communism prevailed in Korea that Japan, the Philippines, and the rest of Southeast Asia would soon follow.[5]

After the passage of the 25-27 June 1950[6] United Nations Security Council Resolutions, the U.S. began deploying combat forces to South Korea. The first combat forces to arrive consisted of the 403 men of 'Task Force Smith' who arrived on 1 July 1950[7] and substantially increased during the three year war peaking, at 326,863 in 1953.[8]

The war was costly for all nations involved. The U.S. suffered 33,629 deaths, 23,300 killed in action (KIA), and 105,785 wounded in action (WIA); ROK forces suffered 47,000 KIA and 183,000 WIA; other United Nations forces suffered 3,194 KIA and 11,297 WIA; and communist forces suffered over 1,000,000 casualties. Additionally, there were roughly 1,000,000 South Korean civilian casualties and 1,000,000 North Korean civilian casualties.[9] An armistice ending hostilities was signed on 27 July, 1953. On 1 October, 1953, the U.S. and South Korea entered into a Mutual Defense Treaty (MDT). This treaty states that if either country is attacked by a third country, the U.S. and South Korea will act together to defend one another.[10] In support of this treaty, the U.S. has continued to station military forces in South Korea for the past 60 years. The number of U.S. troops stationed in South Korea has steadily decreased as the capacity of the South Korean military to defend its country has increased. During the late 1950s and 1960s, U.S. troop levels in South Korea hovered around 60,000.[11]

In 1971 the United States reduced the number of U.S. forces in South Korea by approximately 1/3 (withdrawing 20,000 of the 62,000 then stationed there). This reduction (made despite Seoul's protest) was the result of the 'Nixon Doctrine' calling for America's Asian allies to provide for more of their own defense.[12] Minor reductions in the number of U.S. forces stationed in South Korea continued during the Carter, George H. Bush, Clinton, and George W. Bush administrations. The last significant reduction took place when the 2nd Brigade Combat Team from the 2nd Infantry Division deployed from Korea to Iraq for Operation Iraqi Freedom in August 2004. A year later, the BCT redeployed to the United States rather than return to South Korea.[13] Today there are approximately 28,500 United States service members stationed in South Korea serving alongside 650,000 South Korean military troops.[14] These troops provide a tripwire and serve as an "unequivocal symbol of the U.S. defense commitment"[15] to South Korea.

Questioning the Continued Stationing of Troops in South Korea. The debate over whether or not it is in the best interests of the U.S. to station forces in South Korea has been going on for many years, even before the end of the Cold War. In addition to the aforementioned Nixon Doctrine released in 1971, soon after taking office in 1977, President Carter announced his desire to significantly reduce and ultimately eliminate the U.S. footprint in South Korea. Despite his stated intention, he did not do so because of increased concerns about the North Korean threat after the discovery of tunnels under the Demilitarized Zone.[16]

The end of the Cold War caused the U.S. to again reexamine its commitment to forward deploy U.S. forces in South Korea. The administrations of George H. Bush and Bill Clinton desired to reduce U.S. forces in South Korea, but decided against doing so because of increased anxiety over North Korea's nuclear weapons program.[17] Most recently, President George W. Bush announced in August 2004 his plan to withdraw 70,000 military personnel from Germany and South Korea, stating "The world has changed a great deal and our posture must change with it."[18]

The continued stationing of U.S. forces in South Korea after the conclusion of the Cold War has been called an anachronistic commitment by some. In addition to the demise of the Soviet Union, it is argued that South Korea is no longer in a position where it requires U.S. forces to deter or defend itself from an attack by North Korea. While North Korea still maintains a large military, it is one equipped with weapon systems developed in the 1950s and 1960s. The ROK military, on the other hand, possesses modern weapon systems and is superior to the North Korean military in readiness, command and control systems, and training. Furthermore, South Korea's Gross Domestic Product (GDP) ranks 12th in the world and is 40 times greater than that of North Korea, its population is twice as large, and it is technologically superior to North Korea.[19]

The current economic challenges the U.S. faces has further intensified this debate. It is an issue being addressed in the U.S. Congress, in the current presidential race, and in academia.

On 11 May 2011 members of the US Senate Armed Services Committee (SASC) Carl Levin, John McCain, and James Webb called on the U.S. to relook the proposed military realignments it is executing with South Korea and Japan.[20] While this request to reexamine these military realignments does not directly request a reduction in military forces in South Korea, any comprehensive evaluation of these plans will require an examination of the level of U.S. troops stationed there.

Republican Presidential candidate (and former ambassador to China) Jon Huntsman called for cutting the active duty Army and transferring more missions to the Army Reserve and Guard. He also proposed closing at least 50 military installations overseas in order to save costs and to better structure the U.S. military for post Cold War capabilities.[21]

Richard Kohn, professor emeritus of history and peace, war, and defense at the University of North Carolina at Chapel Hill, has stated that 20 years after the end of the Cold War it's time for the U.S. to revise its policy and strategy and to revise our military force structure. This includes an honest reassessment of the number of U.S. forces that must be based overseas.[22]

U.S. Interests in the Region

The stability of the Pacific region has always been a vital interest to the United States. This has never been truer than today as the region is becoming increasingly

5

important to the world economy. The Asia-Pacific region contains approximately 50% of the world's population including the two countries with the largest populations, China and India, as well as nine of the world's twenty largest cities. The region contains approximately 37% of the world's GDP along with many of the world's fastest growing economies. China alone has doubled its per capita GDP in the past 11 years.[23] Additionally, five of the world's seven largest militaries belong to nations in the region.

The increased importance the U.S. places on the Asian-Pacific region is reflected in recent comments by senior American leaders. Secretary of State Hillary Clinton has declared that the U.S. is now in "America's Pacific Century."[24] President Obama recently reinforced the importance of the region in a speech he made in New Zealand when he stated "The United States is a Pacific power and we are here to stay."[25] President Obama further stated "The Asia-Pacific is critical to achieving my highest priority, and that's creating jobs and the opportunity for the American people…with most of the world's nuclear powers and half of humanity, Asia will largely define whether the century ahead will be marked by conflict or cooperation."[26]

The goal of the United States in the region is to promote continued regional stability. The stability guaranteed by U.S. military forces forward deployed in the region has been one of the major factors that has allowed for significant economic growth in Asia since the end of World War II, including in China during the past 10 years. The potential for continued growth in the region is dependent on this continued regional stability. In order to provide this regional stability, the U.S. is committed to maintaining a forward based presence in the region.[27] This commitment is important to U.S. allies in the region. Secretary Clinton made this very clear when she stated:

6

Beyond our borders, people are also wondering about America's intentions – our willingness to remain engaged and to lead. In Asia, they ask whether we are really there to stay, whether we are likely to be distracted again by the events elsewhere, and whether we can back those commitments with action. The answer is: We can, and we will. Strategically, maintaining peace and security across the Asia-Pacific is increasingly crucial to global progress, whether through defending freedom of navigation in the South China Sea, countering the proliferation efforts of North Korea, or ensuring transparency in the military activities of the region's key players. Just as Asia is critical to America's future, an engaged America is vital to Asia's future.[28]

The importance the U.S. places on its alliances in the region to promote regional security is clearly laid out in the 2010 National Security Strategy (NSS). The NSS states:

> Our alliances with Japan, South Korea, Australia, the Philippines, and Thailand are the bedrock of security in Asia and a foundation of prosperity in the Asia-Pacific region. We will continue to deepen and update these alliances to reflect the dynamism of the region and strategic trends of the 21st Century. Japan and South Korea are increasingly important leaders in addressing regional and global issues, as well as in embodying and promoting our common democratic values. We are modernizing our security relationships with both countries to face evolving 21st century global security challenges and to reflect the principle of equal partnership with the United States and to ensure a sustainable foundation for the U.S. military presence there. We are working together with our allies to develop a positive security agenda for the region, focused on regional security, combating the proliferation of weapons of mass destruction, terrorism, climate change, international piracy, epidemics, and cyber security, while achieving balanced growth and human rights.[29]

Security Relations and the South Korea – United States Alliance

The United States and South Korea have been staunch allies since the start of the Korean War. In addition to the security framework established with the 1953 Mutual Defense Treaty, the U.S. provides South Korea with a 'nuclear umbrella' as an extended deterrent measure.[30] The focus of the security alliance has evolved over time. Initially it was focused on the defense of South Korea from a North Korean attack and on the U.S. Cold War communist containment policy. Today there are many factors that shape the alliance. These include: 1) The North Korean threat to South Korea, its

development and proliferation of weapons of mass destruction, and its risk of collapse;

2) The desire of South Korea to play a greater regional role; 3) China's ascent to world

power and its rising regional and global influence; 4) South Korea's development of a

strong export-oriented industrial base that has allowed it to become one of the world's

leading economies; and 5) South Korea's maturing democracy and the role public

opinion plays in Seoul's foreign policy.[31]

In addition to working together to maintain South Korea's security on the Korean

Peninsula, South Korea has been one of the United States' most reliable allies,

supporting U.S. military operations around the world. South Korea deployed two

divisions to Vietnam in support of U.S. military operations in the 1960s and more

recently deployed 3,000 Soldiers to Iraq and 300 to Afghanistan to serve in noncombat

roles in support of U.S. operations in these countries.[32]

Role of U.S. Troops stationed in South Korea

Of the 28,500 U.S. military personnel serving in South Korea today,

approximately 17,940 (63%) are U.S. Army personnel.[33] The remaining 10,500 military

personnel are Sailors, Airmen, and Marines. These forces are provided "to Combined

Forces Command (CFC)/ United States Forces Korea (USFK) to deter aggression

against the Republic of Korea (ROK), and should deterrence fail, to defeat that

aggression."[34] The majority of the Soldiers serving in Korea fall under the Eighth U.S.

Army (EUSA) and its subordinate commands. These troops are stationed in Korea to

support the U.S. goal of ensuring continued regional security. The primary threats to

continued regional security are North Korea and uncertainties caused by the rise of

China.

North Korean Threat. North Korea has the potential to significantly threaten stability in the region. The North Korean regime believes it faces major security concerns from both external sources as well as serious internal threats. Because of these threats, North Korean leaders understand they are in a struggle for their survival. In order to protect its survival, Kim Jong-il (KJI) adopted the concept of *Songun* (military first) which places the military at the center of the state and the political process in the country.[35] This policy justifies a military force consisting of 1.1 million active personnel along with a reserve force of approximately 4.7 million. Approximately 31% of the North Korean GDP is used to sustain the force.[36] This posture coupled with North Korea's isolation has resulted in a country with "little connection to the global economy and few institutional links"[37] making it difficult to influence, understand, and predict decisions that will be made by its leaders.[38]

The threat to regional security posed by the Democratic People's Republic of Korea (DPRK) falls into three areas. First is an attack into South Korea (either a full scale attack with the intent of reunifying the country or more limited provocative attacks), second is its development and proliferation of weapons of mass destruction, and third is its collapse.

North Korean Attack. Most leading experts concur that an attack by North Korea against South Korea to reunify the country by force is unlikely. The DPRK has stated that it will not launch a first strike and will only use military force to defend itself. Furthermore, preservation of power and of the regime is the highest priority for North Korean leadership and they appear to clearly acknowledge that a full scale attack against South Korea would result in the end of their regime.[39]

Other reasons that make an attack unlikely is the DPRK view that the people of South Korea and North Korea are one, the economic potential of the South, and the inability of North Korea to sustain an attack into the South without external support. The economic strength of the South has become evident and important to North Korea in the recent past as South Koreans have made continued efforts to increase economic support to the North.[40]

While a full scale attack by the North is unlikely, it cannot be discounted. If the DPRK felt that an attack against it was imminent or if an attack was required to prevent the collapse of the regime, then it might be compelled to attack the South in one 'last ditch' effort.[41] Additionally, the DPRK has employed limited, calculated military force against the ROK as recently as 2010. In March 2010, the DPRK killed 46 ROK sailors when they torpedoed a South Korean Naval Ship, the *Cheonan*. Then on November 23, the DPRK launched an artillery attack against the South Korean Island of Yeonpyeong. The attack using approximately 170 artillery shells resulted in the death of two ROK Marines. Additionally, 18 Marines and three civilians were wounded.[42] These limited attacks appear to have been carefully calculated to garner internal support within North Korea while not being so provocative or egregious as to cause a significant response by South Korea. The lack of a ROK response to the Yeonpyeong attack resulted in the resignation of the ROK defense minister, Kim Tae-Young. South Koreans citizens have demanded a stronger response to any similar North Korean provocation in the future. As a result, South Korea has modified its rules of engagement, which in the past were crafted to safeguard against escalation, to allow a much more forceful response in the future.[43] Consequently, similar future provocations by North Korea may cause an unanticipated response by South Korea that could escalate into a full scale confrontation between the two countries.

The presence of U.S. military forces stationed in South Korea unquestionably has stabilized the region and contributed significantly to the fact there has not been large scale fighting between North and South Korea since the end of the Korean War. The deterrent value of these U.S. forces has diminished over the years as U.S. forces in South Korea down-sized, the capability of the ROK military increased, and the support provided to North Korea by China and Russia decreased as the Cold War ended. Still, today "America's presence undoubtedly still helps deter the DPRK from military adventurism."[44]

The question is whether or not the deterrence provided by the U.S. has to include the continued stationing of forces in South Korea. This is not an easy question to answer. Many conclude that South Korea is fully capable of defending itself and defeating a North Korean attack. They state that "South Korea can stand on its own."[45] They reference a 2002 Center for Strategic and International Studies (CSIS) report that concluded the ROK is able to defend itself against an attack by North Korea to support their argument that the U.S. should withdraw forces from South Korea.[46] The fact that western experts estimate South Korea can defend itself against an attack by North Korea does not address the deterrence provided by U.S. forces stationed in South Korea. It is not simply enough to defeat an attack once it begins; what is important is to prevent (deter) it from ever occurring in the first place. A successful defense by South Korea would still create a great deal of regional instability with results that cannot be predicted.

The question we have to consider is whether or not the capability of the ROK military (with off peninsula support the U.S. would provide) is enough to deter the DPRK from aggression. It is doubtful that the DPRK draws the same conclusion that CSIS and others have about South Korea's ability to defeat a DPRK attack by itself. Is the additional deterrence provided by U.S. forces in South Korea required to prevent aggression by the North? These are difficult questions to answer given the lack of transparency inside North Korea and the unpredictability of DPRK leadership. What is clear, given the two limited North Korean attacks in 2010, is that North Korea is willing to use military force against the South in a manner calculated to achieve its objectives without risking full scale war. While some might argue the North Koreans would not have engaged in these limited attacks if U.S. forces were not stationed in South Korea, there is little evidence to support this. It is, however, logical to conclude that the presence of U.S. forces in South Korea in conjunction with ROK military forces provides a greater deterrent against DPRK military action than would ROK forces by themselves. If these U.S. forces were not present, the DPRK might gamble on whether or not the U.S. would act in defense of the ROK. The U.S. troops deployed in South Korea "carry the most indisputable symbol of (this) commitment."[47]

The continued presence of American forces and the U.S. commitment they represent also serves as a calming influence to prevent South Korean forces from responding disproportionately to provocation by the DPRK that could lead to a full scale conflict. It is also logical to assume that the presence of U.S. forces in South Korea influences China to strongly encourage DPRK restraint from creating a military crisis on the peninsula.

12

North Korean Weapons of Mass Destruction. North Korea's acquisition of nuclear weapons has had serious implications for regional stability despite the efforts of regional powers through the six-party talks and it is unlikely that the DPRK will willingly give up this capability. In addition to concerns over North Korea having these weapons, there is also a great deal of concern over its willingness to share this technology with other nations and non-state actors.

North Korea detonated its first nuclear weapon in an underground test on 9 October, 2006. U.S. intelligence soon confirmed this successful detonation, reported to be less than 1 kiloton. This, coupled with advances in the DPRK missile program that provides it the capability to strike throughout the region as well as Alaska and the continental United States, causes great concern. Evidence of this concern is that North Korea's staunchest ally, China issued strong warnings to North Korea not to conduct nuclear weapons testing when it became apparent it was preparing to do so. "When North Korea tested the devices nonetheless, Chinese leaders were furious and supported UN sanctions."[48]

It is difficult to fully understand the reasons behind North Korea's acquisition of nuclear weapons. Possible reasons include drawing the focus and attention of the United States to North Korea, to counter the internal unrest that might be caused by the deteriorating economic conditions in North Korea, concern over being identified as a part of the 'Axis of Evil' by U.S. President George W. Bush and concern that they would be next in line for regime change after Iraq, and to coerce the U.S. to negotiate.[49]

Regardless of its rationale for developing these weapons, now that North Korea has acquired them, it is unlikely it will willingly divest of them unless it can be convinced it is in its best interest to do so. DPRK leadership appears to believe the ownership of nuclear weapons is essential to their survival. "According to Han S. Park, North Koreans are convinced that it is their military capability and possession of nuclear weapons that prevents the U.S. from invading. As a result, in the minds of the public in North Korea, the bomb itself is a product of *songun*, and *songun* will continue to deter U.S. aggression."[50] This belief that nuclear weapons are essential to the survival of the North Korean regime has been reinforced in the eyes of the DPRK by what they have seen happen to Saddam Hussein's regime in Iraq and Muammar Gaddafi's regime in Libya.[51] On 22 March, 2011 three days after the U.S. joined other western powers in air attacks against Libyan forces loyal to Gaddafi, a DPRK spokesman issued the following statement:

> The present Libyan crisis teaches the international community a serious lesson.   It was fully exposed before the world that "Libya's nuclear dismantlement" much touted by the U.S. in the past turned out to be a mode of aggression whereby the latter coaxed the former with such sweet words as 'guarantee of security' and 'improvement of relations' to disarm itself and then swallowed it up by force. It proved once again the truth of history that peace can be preserved only when one builds up one's own strength as long as highhanded and arbitrary practices go on in the world. The DPRK was quite just when it took the path of *Songun* and the military built up this course serves as a very valuable deterrent for averting a war and defending peace and stability on the Korean Peninsula.[52]

Despite the desire of the U.S. and other regional partners for North Korea to give up its weapons, it is unrealistic to believe this will take place in the foreseeable future given North Korea's perception of the importance of these weapons to its survival. Instead of focusing on getting North Korea to give up its weapons, it is more prudent to focus efforts on the prevention of North Korean proliferation of this technology and of preventing North Korean weapons from falling into the wrong hands during a potential regime collapse.

At this point it is irrelevant whether or not U.S. forces in South Korea contributed to North Korea's desire to acquire nuclear weapons. Instead, we must look at the relevance of U.S. forces on the peninsula now that North Korea has these weapons.

U.S. forces stationed in South Korea could possibly be used as a bargaining chip to encourage North Korea to give up its nuclear weapons. The U.S. and South Korea could agree to remove U.S. forces off the peninsula if the DPRK agreed to eliminate its nuclear weapons and submit to inspections. There have also even been calls in South Korea for the U.S. to redeploy or threaten to redeploy nuclear weapons to South Korea (it is believed the last U.S. nuclear weapons were removed from South Korea in 1991) or for South Korea to develop its own nuclear weapons capability to be used as a bargaining chip to encourage North Korea to give up its weapons program.[53]

Previous efforts and agreements to curb North Korean efforts to attain nuclear weapons failed. North Korea agreed in 1994 to halt work toward developing the capacity to produce nuclear weapons as part of the U.S.- North Korea Agreed Framework. This agreement included the provision for the DPRK to remain a party to the nuclear nonproliferation treaty. Despite this agreement, the DPRK continued a clandestine uranium enrichment program.[54] In late 2002 the Agreed Framework was nullified and on 10 January, 2003 North Korea announced its withdrawal from the Nuclear Nonproliferation Treaty.[55]

U.S. forces stationed in South Korea deter the DPRK from using its weapons against South Korea. Just as it is unlikely for North Korea to conduct a conventional attack against South Korea it is unlikely it would conduct an attack using nuclear weapons for many of the same reasons. South Korea would continue to be protected by the U.S. nuclear umbrella in accordance with existing treaties even if there were no U.S. forces on the peninsula. However, it's difficult to predict how North Korea would interpret a unilateral withdrawal of U.S. forces and how it would factor this into its calculations. What is certain is that U.S. forces on the peninsula signal a higher degree of U.S. commitment and therefore serve a greater deterrent affect than if they were not stationed there.

Another consideration that must be taken into account is how the South Koreans would view a withdrawal of U.S. forces from the peninsula while North Korea continued to possess nuclear weapons. Even though they are covered by the U.S. nuclear umbrella, South Koreans might feel compelled to pursue nuclear weapons of their own were not U.S. forces present in South Korea. It is also likely that Japan would feel compelled to acquire nuclear weapons if there were concerns about U.S. commitment to the region.

Two other considerations that must be taken into account are the ability of U.S. forces stationed in South Korea to monitor North Korean activities associated with the use or proliferation of nuclear technology and the potential use of U.S. forces to assist in preventing North Korean nuclear weapons from falling into the wrong hands in the event of the collapse of the North Korea regime. The classification of U.S. capabilities and intentions prevents a detailed analysis of these considerations in this paper.

Collapse of North Korea. "What is more dangerous than a strong dictatorship, a collapsed one."[56] The unexpected and rapid collapse of the DPRK regime could potentially have a major destabilizing effect on the region. It could include a large influx of refugees into South Korea, China, and Russia. It could result in an armed civil war inside North Korea between those supporting the regime and those against. The resultant humanitarian catastrophe in a country already facing humanitarian crisis could be immense.[57] The North Korean people, who are already undernourished, receive about half of their food from the government. A disruption in the food supply could result in mass starvation and a huge refugee flow. The humanitarian crisis will become more severe the longer people are forced to go without food and medicine. This may cause the refugee problem to spread beyond Korea, cause a civil war or insurgency, and increase the risk that North Korea's weapons of mass destruction might end up on the international black market.[58]

The collapse of North Korea would potentially have huge impacts to the South Korean economy as evidenced when the two Germanys reunited at the conclusion of the Cold War. It could place South Korea, China, the United States Russia, and Japan in a "chaotic situation where there has been little regional planning....and could result in creating an unstable, nuclear armed regime raising questions about command and control of these weapons and the dangers of proliferation."[59]

The collapse of the North Korean regime is a very real concern to DPRK leaders. Internal DPRK issues include the estimated starvation of up to 4 million people since 1995 and the estimated 6 million North Koreans at risk of starvation today.[60] The recent death of Kim Jong-il (KJI) has created a great deal of uncertainty about the ability of the regime to endure. The regime is now attempting to transfer leadership of the regime to KJI's 28 year old son Kim, Jong-un (KJU). While KJI was 70 years old and had suffered from declining health for some time "little had been done to prepare KJU or the North Korean people for this succession, making it unclear whether the central government in Pyongyang will be able to maintain stability"[61] during the transition of power. Succeeding a dictator is a very difficult challenge because it takes time for the new leader to consolidate power. KJI was afforded ample time, about 15 years, to consolidate power prior to the death of his father Kim, Il-sung (KIS). This provided him time to "advance his friends and purge enemies and create a personality cult to promote his legitimacy as heir."[62] The sudden death of KJI may not have afforded KJU the opportunity to secure enough power to be able to rule North Korea successfully.[63] The extreme hardship in North Korea, where many are on the verge of starvation, will complicate KJU's ascension to power while so young and untested in a society that places a premium on age and experience.

Events associated with the Arab Spring appear to have raised additional awareness within the DPRK of its susceptibility to internal unrest. This is evidenced by reports that numerous North Korean doctors and nurses have been stranded in Libya following the death of Gadhafi as well as doctors, nurses, and technicians working in Tunisia and Egypt. These personnel were sent overseas to earn money that was sent back to North Korea to support the regime. Now that these North Koreans have witnessed the internal unrest leading to the overthrow of dictatorships, North Korean leaders do not want to allow them to return to the country and be able to talk about this. The tight control placed on North Korean media has prevented any reporting of these uprisings within the country. It has been estimated that fewer than 1% of North Koreans are aware of the Arab Spring. DPRK officials' denial of North Koreans who witnessed these events from returning home is an attempt to maintain this ignorance.[64]

There are three considerations stationing U.S. military personnel in South Korea have in relation with the collapse of the DPRK. The first is that the presence of U.S. Soldiers does support the DPRK's policy of *Songun*. North Korea uses the U.S. presence for propaganda purposes to rally the people of North Korea to accept sacrifices associated with so much of their GDP being used to prop up the regime and support the military. The North Korean regime is able to point to the presence of U.S. military personnel in South Korea as an imminent threat to their nation. North Korea consistently issues press releases about the semi-annual exercises conducted in South Korea (Ulchi-Freedom Guardian and Key Resolve) to assert that the U.S. and South Koreans are planning to attack North Korea. This supports their continued reliance on *Songun* to protect the nation. While one would expect this imminent threat would lead to a 'cry-wolf syndrome' after 60 years, the North is able to point to the preparedness of its military forces as the reason the wolf has been kept at bay. The second consideration is that while *Songun* may be bad for the people of North Korea, it does ensure stability in North Korea. This is good from a regional security and stability perspective given the potential instability that would be caused by a sudden collapse of the DPRK. A stable DPRK that gradually reforms from within, similar to China and Vietnam, may in fact be the best scenario for the region. The third consideration is that the presence of U.S. forces in South Korea best postures U.S. forces to assist others in the region in responding to a sudden collapse to address a humanitarian crises and issues associated with the DPRK's weapons of mass destruction.

Rise of China. The rise of Chinese economic and military power in East Asia has created challenges for the United States. China's lack of military transparency especially with regard to its naval capabilities is a growing concern for all nations in the region and has the potential for reducing regional stability.[65] These challenges are so significant that U.S. Secretary of State Hillary Clinton has stated "China represents one of the most challenging and consequential bilateral relationships the United States has ever had to manage. This calls for careful, steady, dynamic stewardship, an approach to China on our part that is grounded in reality, focused on results, and true to our principles and interests."[66] While U.S. official policy is that it welcomes China's rise, it is also clear that the United States is closely monitoring potential security threats associated with China's increased military capability. As a result, the U.S. security strategy in East Asia has consistently included engaging China to encourage it to become a stakeholder in the existing international system while at the same time enhancing its regional security alliances to deter China militarily. Through this approach the U.S. has attempted to maintain the regional balance of power to promote stability and reassure its regional allies.[67]

It is clear that U.S. forward deployed forces in the Pacific, such as those stationed in South Korea, have contributed to regional stability in the past. But will they continue to do so in the future or will they become a potential point of friction between the U.S. and China as China's power continues to grow? It is difficult to assess the future, but currently there appears to be little cause for concern that forward deployed U.S. forces in South Korea are a point of friction between the U.S. and China. In fact, it is likely China prefers to have U.S. forces in South Korea given shared concerns over North Korea. Some believe "that Beijing may prefer to maintain a divided Korean Peninsula out of fear that a unified Korea may lead to greater instability in the region.

Strategically, North Korea is currently a buffer between China and the democratic influence of Japan and South Korea."[68] While there is debate amongst different Chinese thinkers about policies China should adopt regarding Sino-North Korean issues, the top priority of current policy is to maintain stability and peace on the peninsula. Current Chinese policy also concludes that it is too early for a unified Korea and that this should only be achieved by peaceful means.[69]

China's rise is a significant concern for other nations in the region and the presence of U.S. forces promotes stability by reassuring them of the U.S. commitment to maintaining regional security. It is also clear that the presence of the U.S. forces in the region reassures our allies, causes them less concern about Chinese intentions, and prevents a possible arms race in the region. This concern over China establishing a regional hegemony is reflected in a Chicago Council Global Affairs survey that concluded "only 10 percent of Japanese, 21 percent of South Koreans, and 27 percent of Indonesians would be comfortable with China as the future leader in Asia."[70] Further evidence of concern over China's rise in the region was the announcement President Obama made during a November 2011 trip to Australia stating the U.S. and Australia had agreed to "expand military cooperation between the long time allies and boost America's presence in the region."[71] This agreement includes sending 250 Marines to Australia for exercises and training and the deployment of a full Marine ground task force over the next several years.[72]

Concerns With Continued Stationing of U.S. Forces in the Republic of Korea

There are three major arguments made by those that advocate removing U.S. forces from South Korea. The first is that U.S. forces in South Korea are committed to the peninsula and are unavailable for contingencies elsewhere in the world. This is an increasing concern as the U.S. military down-sizes, since the U.S wants to maintain strategic flexibility with its military force. The second issue is the cost of stationing forces in South Korea, especially with the current economic concerns in the U.S. The third issue is increased South Korea resentment of the continued presence of U.S forces in their country.

Strategic Flexibility. Reductions in U.S. military forces following the end of the Cold War coupled with the focus placed on combating international terrorism following the September 2011 attacks has increased the desire of the U.S. to have more strategic flexibility with its armed forces (troops stationed and committed to South Korea have in the past been viewed as unavailable to respond to crisis or contingencies elsewhere). This includes the option of deploying forces stationed on the Korean Peninsula to other areas of conflict. The U.S. desire to be able to deploy U.S. forces stationed in South Korea to other parts of the region and world was initially opposed by the Korean government due to concerns of entangling South Korea in conflicts between China and the United States. However, the two countries reached an agreement on this issue in the mid-2000s. As part of this agreement, South Korea acknowledged that the United States can deploy its forces off the Korean Peninsula in support of operations elsewhere. However, U.S. forces cannot operate from South Korea while engaged in conflict with other nations. Any return of U.S. forces to the Korean Peninsula following their deployment is subject to discussion and agreement of both nations.[73]

This agreement affords the U.S. the ability to use U.S. forces in South Korea as part of its global force pool. The deployment of 2nd BCT, 2nd Infantry Division from South Korea to Iraq is an example where the U.S. did in fact do this. Still, there is little doubt that forces stationed in South Korea are not as available for worldwide deployment as those stationed in the United States. Forces in South Korea are considered committed to the defense of South Korea and the U.S. would likely avoid using these forces elsewhere unless there was no other alternative.

Cost of Maintaining U.S. Forces in South Korea. Costs associated with stationing U.S. Forces in South Korea following the Korean War were borne by the U.S. for the first several decades of the alliance. The U.S. began pressuring the ROK to contribute to these costs in the 1980s. After intense negotiations, South Korea agreed to begin contributing cash to share in these costs beginning in 1989. Multi-year cost sharing agreements have been concluded every few years since.[74]

Today, the U.S.-ROK cost sharing agreement requires South Korea to contribute financial support to the United States to offset the cost of stationing U.S. forces in South Korea through 2013. In 2011, the cost of stationing U.S. forces in South Korea was about $1.769B (about what the U.S. spends per week during Operation Enduring Freedom). Of this $1.769B, the U.S. contributed $1.026B. The ROK contributed ~$743M (812.5 billion won), approximately 42% of the cost of stationing U.S. forces on the peninsula. The U.S. desires to see the ROK contribution increase to 50%. Under a cost sharing agreement reached in 2009, the share of the South Korean contributions will increase each year until 2013 in order to achieve a 50% cost share.[75]

Public Resentment of Continued U.S. Presence in South Korea. Resentment over the U.S. presence in South Korea has increased as South Korean military and economic capability has increased. As South Korea has become more self sufficient and self confident, the continued U.S. presence has raised concerns over sovereignty.

This concern for sovereignty falls into two primary areas. One is command and control of ROK military forces. The second is a little more difficult to pinpoint since it has many factors. It has been termed "anti-Americanism" and includes factors such as the perception that U.S. Soldiers guilty of crimes against South Koreans are not held accountable.

Operational Control (OPCON) Transfer. During the Korean War all South Korean military forces came under the Operational Control of U.S. military forces. This relationship of ROK military forces serving under U.S. military command continued until the establishment of Combined Forces Command (CFC) on November 7, 1978. CFC is commanded by a U.S. General who also serves as the Commander of United States Forces Korea (USFK) as well as Commander of United Nations Command. In his role as the CFC Commander, the U.S. General has dual reporting chains to the national authorities of both the U.S. and the ROK. From 1978 to 1994, the CFC Commander commanded ROK military forces in peacetime just as he would in time of war. In 1994, peacetime operational control of ROK military forces was transferred to the South Korean Joint Chiefs of Staff (JCS). In the event of war, OPCON of most South Korean forces would pass back to the CFC Commander (the Second Republic of Korea Army (SROKA) and Capital Defense Command remain under ROK JCS control).[76] Since 1994, the two nations have continued to examine the creation of a command structure that would allow the ROK to retain operational control over its military forces in time of war. An agreement reached in 2007 would have disbanded CFC and established separate U.S. and ROK commands in April 2012. Under this agreement, each country would retain command of its military forces during both peacetime and war time. A command structure will be established that provides a supporting to supported relationship with ROK military forces being the supported command and assuming the lead for the defense of their country with U.S. military forces providing support. A subsequent agreement in June 2010 between U.S. President Barrack Obama and South Korean President Lee, Myung bak delayed OPCON transfer by 3 years. It is now scheduled to take place in 2015.[77]

South Korean resentment of the continued stationing of U.S. troops in South Korea has become a significant concern for the alliance. Polls indicate that the vast majority of South Koreans (approximately 70%) prefer the U.S. to continue to maintain a presence in their country[78] but anti-American resentment ebbs and flows. It is typically higher following violent crimes committed by U.S. service members against South Koreans and is much lower following North Korea provocations. "Kim Sung-Han of the Institute of Foreign Affairs and National Security has stated anti-Americanism is getting intense. It used to be widespread but not so deep. Now it's getting widespread and deep."[79] Many reasons have been given for this anti-Americanism. These include the frustration over the South Korean perceptions that the U.S. does not treat South Korea as an equal partner in the US-ROK security alliance, that the U.S. acts in its own self-interest without regard for the ROK, resentment over the perceived ROK dependence on the U.S. for its security, closer economic ties between the ROK and China, previous U.S. support to authoritarian regimes in South Korea, the role the U.S. played in dividing the peninsula, and the perception that the Status of Forces Agreement (SOFA) is unfair because it allows U.S. personnel in South Korea to commit crimes against South Koreans for which they are not held accountable.

The fact that the majority of South Koreans want the U.S. to maintain a troop presence in their country does not mean they do not harbor anti-American feelings. Anti-American sentiments are different than anti-alliance sentiments. Very "widespread and even violent anti-American movements during Korean democratization in the 1980s took place amid continued support for the alliance."[80] While the majority of South Koreans desire the security afforded by U.S. troops, polls indicate the perception South Korean's have of America itself has declined. "A 1982 poll taken by the Tonga Ilbo (Far Eastern daily), …showed that the country most liked by Koreans was by far the United States (61.6%), and that 58.1% rated South Korea – U.S. relations as satisfactory."[81] Surveys taken in December 1990 indicated that only 38.7% or South Koreans liked the United States while 29.6% disliked it,[82] a significant drop in the South Korean perception of the U.S. in only 8 years. By the 2002 South Korean presidential election, polls indicated that barely 1/3 of South Koreans viewed America favorably while 60% viewed the U.S. unfavorably.[83]

Another aspect of the anti-American / anti-alliance issue is that it appears to be generational. Older Koreans who were alive during the Korean War or who came of age in the 1960s and 1970s prior to the tremendous economic development in South Korea tend to view the presence of American forces very favorably. Younger Koreans (such as the so called 486 generation who are now in their 40s, reached adulthood in the 80s and were born in the 60s) view the presence of U.S. forces much less favorably.[84] A June, 2006 poll taken in South Korea found that 56% of people between the ages of 15 and 19 are in favor of the withdrawal of U.S. troops from South Korea.[85]

Support in the U.S. for the continued stationing of troops in South Korea has remained fairly consistent. A poll conducted by the Princeton Survey Research Association in 2003 indicated that only 19% of those polled in the U.S. wanted U.S. military personnel withdrawn or reduced while 75% wanted troop levels to remain the same or be increased.[86] While there is still strong U.S. support for the continued troop presence in South Korea, this could be significantly eroded by increased anti-Americanism in South Korea.

The U.S. and the ROK have taken steps to address concerns associated with anti-Americanism (such as establishing curfews for American service members and allowing many crimes by U.S. service members to be adjudicated in the South Korean judicial system). Still, this is likely an issue that will continue as long as U.S. forces are stationed in South Korea. While it may be managed, it is unlikely it can be completely eliminated.

Concerns over the continued stationing of U.S. forces in South Korea are valid and the two countries continue to work together to address and mitigate them. Agreements reached in the past 10 years allow the U.S. the strategic flexibility it requires with its force, provides for a 50/50 split on sharing the cost of stationing U.S. forces in Korea, and in 2015 will transfer operational control of ROK military forces back to the ROK JCS in time of war.

Alternatives

While the U.S. is committed to continued engagement in the region, the nature of this engagement must continually be reexamined. Are U.S. combat troops stationed in South Korea necessary to provide the required level of engagement needed to promote regional stability and reassure our allies? Or can the U.S. provide this same level of

27

support and regional stability while reducing the number of troops deployed in South Korea?

The U.S. has three plausible options regarding stationing of troops in South Korea. The first is to continue to maintain the current forces on the peninsula. The second option is to significantly reduce ground combat forces while maintaining air and naval forces currently stationed in South Korea. The third option is to remove all forces from South Korea while continuing to fulfill the requirements of the 1953 MDT with air and naval forces stationed elsewhere in the region along with periodic training exercises involving ground forces. Both Option 2 and 3 would reduce U.S. forces currently stationed in South Korea, save the U.S money, allow these troops to be stationed elsewhere or be cut from the U.S. force structure, and potentially reduce some anti-Americanism is South Korea. However, both could potentially send a message that the U.S. is disengaging from the region.

It is important to note that none of these options call for the U.S. to withdraw from the MDT or completely disengage from the region. It is well established policy that stability in the Asia-Pacific is vital to the United States. Secretary of State Hillary Clinton has stated publically that "One of the most important tasks of American statecraft over the next decade will therefore be to lock in a substantially increased investment – diplomatic, economic, strategic, and otherwise – in the Asia-Pacific."[87]

Alternative #1 (Maintain Current Forces Stationed in South Korea). This option would retain the 28,500 Soldiers, Sailors, Airmen, and Marines stationed in South Korea. This force posture is the most expensive of the three but also provides the greatest flexibility to react to crisis on the peninsula or in the region as well as the greatest deterrence. This alternative continues to provide forces available to support a wide range of ground contingencies on the peninsula even as the alliance continues judicious recalibration such as the disbandment of CFC in 2015. These contingencies include providing support to the ROK military during the collapse of the North Korean regime, providing security to U.S. Air Force bases or other governmental facilities, and assisting with Noncombatant Evacuation Operations (NEO) of U.S. citizens. This alternative provides a forward deployed BCT that is available for deployment regionally to support U.S. contingency operations. Additionally, the continued forward basing of these combat troops signals the resolve of the United States to continue to strongly support its South Korean ally and remain engaged in the region. This is a signal not only to South Korea and our other regional allies, but also to North Korea and China.

Alternative #2 (Remove U.S. Ground Combat Troops from South Korea While Leaving Air Force and Naval Personnel on the Peninsula). In 2007, along with the decision to disband CFC, the United States announced that in the future the U.S. force's role in South Korea would be primarily to provide Air and Naval support to the South Korean armed forces. The ROK active military forces consist of about 681,000 personnel. Of these 550,000 are in the ROK Army and the ROK Navy and Air Force contain about 65,000 apiece.[88] This alternative would reduce the U.S. footprint in South Korea by approximately 8,000 to 10,000 Soldiers while still retaining an adequate planning staff along with command, control, and support of Naval and Air operations. With U.S. military personnel still stationed on South Korean soil, the U.S. visible commitment to the MDT and engagement in the region would remain intact. While the U.S. would have combat forces in Hawaii and Okinawa (until Marines stationed there are moved to Guam) along with the small force planned for deployment in Australia, the reduction of this BCT might cause some nations in the region to question the strength of this commitment. The redeployment of this BCT would reduce the ability of U.S. forces in South Korea to react to contingencies on the Korean Peninsula. Additionally, the removal of this BCT from South Korea could potentially reduce the strategic flexibility the U.S. currently has with the ability to deploy combat ground forces in the region. The most important factor to consider is the signal this BCT reduction would send to North Korea. The deterrence provided by this BCT (and associated U.S. commitment) to prevent a North Korean limited or full scale attack is something that must be considered. While difficult to measure, it is certain there would be an increased risk of a North Korean miscalculation associated with the removal of the only remaining U.S. BCT in South Korea.

Alternative #3 (Remove all U.S. Forces from South Korea While Continuing to Pledge Full Support to the Defense of South Korea IAW the MDT. This would have to be a phased alternative with some U.S. forces remaining in South Korea until CFC is disbanded in 2015. This option would allow the U.S. to fulfill its treaty obligation to assist in the defense of South Korea and subsequent agreements by providing Air and Naval support to South Korean Forces defending their country. However, it would provide no permanent U.S. forces in South Korea to protect U.S. interests. It would also be viewed by many nations as a U.S. withdrawal from the region. The potential impact to regional stability is difficult to gauge. Clearly there would be increased risk of DPRK provocation because of the significantly reduced deterrent effect. Another potential outcome is that it might cause U.S. allies in the region to more closely align themselves with China. It could also spark an arms race as traditional U.S. allies in the region such as Japan, South Korea, and Taiwan increase their ability to defend themselves since they perceive they can no longer count on U.S. support. This could even include their pursuit of nuclear weapons.

Recommendation and Conclusion

The U.S. should maintain the current level of forces deployed in South Korea (Alternative #1). These forces are part of the strong U.S.-ROK alliance and serve a critical purpose. They provide a deterrent to the threat posed by North Korea as well as address regional concerns raised by China's rise in power.

Two major potential destabilizing factors are best addressed by maintaining the current level of U.S. forces on the Korean Peninsula. The first is the threat North Korea poses to South Korea through the use of military force and the threat it poses to the region and the world if there were a sudden collapse of its regime. Maintaining the current U.S. troop level provides the greatest deterrent to North Korean aggression and places U.S. forces in the best relative position to respond in a crisis caused by a sudden collapse of the North Korean regime.

The second threat addressed by maintaining current troop levels in South Korea is the threat of instability that could be caused by uncertainty over the rise of China coupled with doubts about U.S. commitment to the region. The presence of U.S. forces in South Korea reassures U.S. regional allies of the continued U.S. commitment to their security and to stability in the region. The reassurance provided by this visible and unambiguous commitment helps prevent a regional arms race that might ensue if regional powers felt they needed to significantly increase their military capability to counter concerns of increased Chinese power. This presence also continues to send a strong message to China of U.S. commitment and serves as a balance in the region to encourage China to ascend to power in a responsible manner.

While the U.S. could continue to remain engaged in the region through its air and naval forces and with periodic ground exercises with nations in the region, any reduction in forward deployed U.S. forces would most likely raise doubts in the region about this U.S. commitment. This might result in a miscalculation and subsequent escalation of force that could lead to conflict and instability with far reaching impacts throughout the world.

Maintaining the current troop level is the most costly of the three alternatives. While expensive, the cost to the U.S. is being off-set by the ROK and will continue to become less expensive (relatively) as the ROK's share of the stationing costs increases to 50% in 2013. The cost of maintaining current troop levels in South Korea is also much less costly to the U.S. than costs associated with instability in the region. Similar to insurance policies, the cheapest option is not necessarily the best.

While there has been a rise in anti-Americanism, it is clear that the vast majority of South Koreans and U.S. citizens still support a U.S. troop presence in South Korea. It is probable that South Korean anti-Americanism will continue to grow as the population ages. It is also probable that anti-American rhetoric and protests will spike in the aftermath of any significant crimes committed by U.S. forces against South Koreans. This is an issue the U.S. and ROK governments must continue to manage.

Just as the alliance has evolved over the past 60 years, it must continue to evolve in the future. Leaders of both nations must continue individually and collectively to address the framework of the alliance and make assessments. As threats associated with North Korea and the rise of China change and as concerns with the alliance modify, the alliance itself must adjust.

With the many changes taking place throughout the region and the world, the continued unambiguous resolve and commitment of the U.S. to the stability of the Asia-Pacific and its allies remains a prudent, cost-effective constant. While the initial reason for stationing U.S. forces in South Korea (to contain the spread of communism) is no longer valid, the U.S. troops stationed in South Korea are not an anachronism. They continue to serve a purpose that is vital to U.S. interests today – their presence serves and promotes stability and continued regional security. This not only benefits the U.S. but also the other nations of the region and the world.

Endnotes

[1] Michael Hickey, *The Korean War: The West Confronts Communism* (Woodstock, NY: The Overlook Press, Peter Mayers Publishers, 2000), 20.

[2] Tim Kane, "Global US Troop Deployment," *Center for Defense Analysis Report, no.* 04-11, (Heritage Center, OCT 27, 2004), 4.

[3] Hickey, *The Korean War: The West Confronts Communism,* 25.

[4] James I. Matray, *Historical Dictionary of the Korean War,* (West port, CT: Greenwood Press, 1991), 3.

[5] Hickey, *The Korean War: The West Confronts Communism,* 37.

[6] Matray, *Historical Dictionary of the Korean War,* 499-500.

[7] Hickey, The *Korean War: The West Confronts Communism,* 45.

[8] Kane, "Global US Troop Deployment", 4.

[9] Matray, *Historical Dictionary of the Korean War,* 553.

[10] Mark E. Manyin, Emma Chanlett-Avery, and Mary Beth Nikitin, *U.S.-South Korea Relations,* R41481 (Washington, DC: U.S. Library of Congress, Congressional Research Service, October 22, 2011), 15.

[11] Kane, "Global US Troop Deployment", 4.

[12] Edward A. Olsen, "Why Keep U.S. Forces in Korea," *Far Eastern Economic Review*, FEB 20, 2003, 166.

[13] Bruce Klinger "Proposed Re-Realignment for Northeast Asia Ignores Strategic Realities," May 18, 2011. *The Heritage Foundation WEBMEMO no., 3262*, http://www.heritage.org/research/reports/2011/05/proposed-re-realignment-for-northeast-asia-ignores-strategic-realities (accessed December 9, 2011).

[14] Manyin, Chanlett-Avery, and Nikitin, *U.S.-South Korea Relations*, R41481, 8.

[15] Victor D. Cha, "America's Alliances In Asia: The Coming "Identity Crisis" With The Republic of Korea" in *Recalibrating The U.S. – Republic of Korea Alliance,* Donald W. Boose, Jr., et al (U.S. Army War College Strategic Studies Institute, Carlisle PA, May 2003), 18.

[16] Olsen, "Why Keep U.S. Forces in Korea," 166.

[17] Ibid.

[18] Kane, "Global US Troop Deployment", 2

[19] Doug Bandow, "Ending the Anachronistic Korean Commitment," *Parameters* 33, no. 2 (Summer 2003): 78.

[20] Klinger, "Proposed Re-Realignment for Northeast Asia Ignores Strategic Realities".

[21] E.D. Cain "Jon Huntsman's Vision For The U.S. Military," 24 November 2011, *Forbes*, http://www.forbes.com/sites/erikkain/2011/11/24/jon-huntsmans-vision-for-the-us-military/. (accessed December 6, 2011).

[22] Richard H. Kohn "Kohn to Defense Chicken Littles: It's time to trim defense spending, and here is how," 1 DEC 2011. http://ricks.foreignpolicy.com/posts/2011/12/01/kohn_to_defense_chicken_littles_its_time_to_trim_spending_and_here_is_how (accessed December 6,2011)

[23] Jean-Claude Trichet "The Growing Importance of the Asia-Pacific Region", Speech at New Year's Reception Asia-Pacific 2008 of the German-Asian Business Circle, Frankfurt am Main, 25 February 2008. http://www.ecb.int/press/key/date/2008/html/sp080225.en.html (accessed December 6, 20110).

[24] Hillary Clinton "America's Pacific Century," *Foreign Policy 189*, November 2011, 56-63.

[25] Barack Obama "US President Stresses Importance of Asia-Pacific to U.S." 17 November 2011. *Radio New Zealand News*, http://www.radiaz.co.nz/news/world/91333/us-president-stresses-importance-of-asia-pacific-to-us (accessed December 9, 2011).

[26] Ibid.

[27] Clinton "America's Pacific Century", 58.

[28] Ibid., 57.

[29] Barack Obama, *National Security Strategy*, (Washington, D.C.: The White House, May 2010), 42.

[30] Manyin, Chanlett-Avery, and Nikitin, *U.S.-South Korea Relations*, R41481, 15.

[31] Ibid., 6.

[32] Ibid., 7-8.

[33] United States Army War College, *Army Brief (Theater Strategy and Campaigning),* Dec 4, 2011, slide 2.

[34] John A. Bonin, *Army Employment Data*, (United States Army War College, Carlisle Barracks, PA, SEP 2011), 19.

[35] Terrance Roehrig, "Creating the Conditions for Peace in Korea: Promoting Incremental Change In North Korea," *Korea Observer* 40, no..1 (Spring 2009): 203.

[36] William Boik, "Understanding the North Korean Problem: Why it has become the "Land of Lousy Options," *The Letort Papers* (U.S. Army War College Strategic Studies Institute, Carlisle PA, July 2011), ix.

[37] Roehrig, "Creating the Conditions for Peace in Korea: Promoting Incremental Change In North Korea," 203.

[38] Ibid.

[39] Boik, "Understanding the North Korean Problem: Why it has become the "Land of Lousy Options," 21.

[40] Ibid., 22.

[41] Ibid.

[42] Thomas R. Eddlem "North Korea Attacks South Korea," November 24, 2010. *The New American*, http://thenewamerican.com/index.php/world-mainmenu-33/5292-north-korea-attacks-south-korea (accessed 17 DEC 2011).

[43] Chris Hogg, "South Korea Defense Minister Resigns Over Deadly Clash," 24 November, 2010. *BBC News Asia-Pacific*, http://www.bbc.co.uk/news/world-asia-pacific-11838750 (accessed 4 FEB, 2012).

[44] Bandow "Ending the Anachronistic Korean Commitment," 80.

[45] Ibid.

[46] Ibid.

[47] Cha, "America's Alliances In Asia: The Coming "Identity Crisis" With The Republic of Korea," 20.

[48] Roehrig, "Creating the Conditions for Peace in Korea: Promoting Incremental Change in North Korea," 204-205.

[49] Boik, "Understanding the North Korean Problem: Why it has become the "Land of Lousy Options," 18-19.

[50] Roehrig, "Creating the Conditions for Peace in Korea: Promoting Incremental Change in North Korea," 208.

[51] Ruediger Frank "Libya Lessons for North Korea: a Case of Déjà vu," 17 December, 2011. *38 North: Informed Analysis of North Korea*, http://38north.org/2011/03/libyan-lessons-for-north-korea (accessed 17 DEC 2011).

[52] Alexander Vorontsov "Libya, North Korea, and the International Nonproliferation Regime," December 17, 2011. *38 North: Informed Analysis of North Korea*, http://38north.org/2011/06/vorontsov061411/ (accessed 17 DEC 2011).

[53] Ralph Cossa "U.S. Nuclear Weapons to South Korea?," 11 February, 2012. *US – Korea Institute at SAIS, 38 North*, http://38north.org/2011/07/rcossa071211/ (accessed 11 FEB, 2012).

[54] Donald W. Boose, Jr., "Introduction: The Alliance Challenged," in *Recalibrating The U.S. – Republic of Korea Alliance.* Donald W. Boose, Jr., et al (U.S. Army War College Strategic Studies Institute, Carlisle PA, May 2003), 4-6.

[55] George Bunn and John B. Rhinelander "NPT Withdrawal: Time For The Security Council to Step In," *Arms Control Today* 35, no.4, May 2005, 17-21.

[56] Jennifer Lind "North Korea's End Heralds The Real Crisis," Interview by Victor Fic, *Asia Times Online*, 13 Dec 2011. http://www.atimes.com/atimes/korea/ML13Dg01.html (accessed 13 DEC 2011).

[57] Roehrig, "Creating the Conditions for Peace in Korea: Promoting Incremental Change in North Korea," 208.

[58] Lind "North Korea's End Heralds The Real Crisis," December 13 2011.

[59] Roehrig, "Creating the Conditions for Peace in Korea: Promoting Incremental Change in North Korea," 208.

[60] Robert Park, "Responsibility to Protect North Korea," December 7, 2011. *Harvard International Review*, http://hir.harvard.edu/print/responsibility-to-protect-in-north-korea (accessed December 9, 2011).

[61] Boik, "Understanding the North Korean Problem: Why it has become the "Land of Lousy Options," 2.

[62] Lind "North Korea's End Heralds The Real Crisis," December 13, 2011.

[63] Ibid.

[64] Fareed Zakaria, "Zakaria: Will the North Koreans Rise Up?," November 14, 2011. *CNN*, http://globalpublicsquare.blogs.com//2011/11/14/zakaria-will-the-north-koreans-rise-up/ (accessed November 30, 2011).

[65] Kei Koga, "The US and East Asian Regional Security Architecture: Building a Regional Security Nexus on Hub-and-spoke," *Asian Perspectives* 35, no. 1 (2011), 2.

[66] Clinton "America's Pacific Century", 58.

[67] Koga, "The US and East Asian Regional Security Architecture: Building a Regional Security Nexus on Hub-and-spoke," 4.

[68] Boik, "Understanding the North Korean Problem: Why it has become the "Land of Lousy Options," 31.

[69] Heungkyu Kim, "From a Buffer Zone To A Strategic Burden: Evolving Sino-North Korean Relations During the Hu Jintao Era," *The Korean Journal of Defense Analysis*, 22, No. 1, (March 2010): 62.

[70] Minxin Pei, "Think Again: Asia's Rise", *Foreign Policy* 173, (July/August 2009): 35.

[71] Don Lothian and Lesa Jenson "Obama Pledges US Military Power in Pacific," November 16, 2011. *CNN*, http://www.cnn.com/2011/11/16/world/asia/Australia-obama-trip/index.html?iref=obnet (accessed November 30, 2011).

[72] Ibid.

[73] Manyin, Chanlett-Avery, and Nikitin, *U.S.-South Korea Relations*, R41481, 19.

[74] Jin-Young Chung, "Cost Sharing For USFK In Transition: Wither The ROK-U.S. Alliance?" in *Recalibrating The U.S. – Republic of Korea Alliance,* Donald W. Boose, Jr., et al (U.S. Army War College, Carlisle PA, May 2003), 39-42.

[75] Manyin, Chanlett-Avery, and Nikitin, *U.S.-South Korea Relations*, R41481, 18.

[76] "U.S. Forces, Korea / Combined Forces Command Combined Ground Component Command (GCC)," *Global Security.Org Military.* http://www.globalsecurity.org/military/agency/dod/usfk.htm (accessed November 13, 2011).

[77] Manyin, Chanlett-Avery, and Nikitin, *U.S.-South Korea Relations*, R41481, 18-19.

[78] Amanda K. Brezina "U.S. Military Presence in the Republic of Korea," *School of Public and Environmental Affairs, SPEA Honors Papers Series* 2, no. 3 (Spring 2008): 28.

[79] Bandow "Ending the Anachronistic Korean Commitment," 79.

[80] Gi-wook Shin and Hilary Jan Izatt, "Anti-American and Anti-Alliance Sentiments in South Korea," *Asian Survey,* 51 no. 6 (Nov/DEC, 2011): 1115.

[81] Gi-Wook Shin, "South Korean Anti-Americanism: A Comparative Perspective," *Asian Survey* 36, no. 8 (August 1996): 793.

[82] Ibid.

[83] Gi-wook Shin and Hilary Jan Izatt "Anti-American and Anti-Alliance Sentiments in South Korea," 1122.

[84] Brezina "U.S. Military Presence in the Republic of Korea," 27.

[85] Cheoleon Lee, "Gallop World Poll: South Korea's Political Dilemma," Sep 22, 2006. http://www.gallup.com/poll/24679/gallup-world-poll-south-korea-political-dilemma.aspx (accessed February,8 2012).

[86] "Korea: North and South," January 3-6 2003. *Knight Rider poll conducted by Princeton Survey Research Associates,* http://www.pollingreport.com/korea.htm (accessed February 8, 2012).

[87] Hillary "America's Pacific Century," 56.

[88] Manyin, Chanlett-Avery, and Nikitin, *U.S.-South Korea Relations*, R41481, 19.

www.ingramcontent.com/pod-product-compliance
Lightning Source LLC
Chambersburg PA
CBHW081802280526
45789CB00008B/2969